Self-Portrait With Family

Self-Portrait With Family

Amaan Hyder

Nine
Arches
Press

Self-Portrait With Family
Amaan Hyder

ISBN: 978-1-916760-08-0
eISBN: 978-1-916760-09-7

Cover artwork: Salman Toor, 'Thunderstorm', 2021.
Oil on panel 30 x 24 inches (76.2 x 61 cm) © Salman Toor;
Courtesy of the artist and Luhring Augustine, New York.
Photo: Farzad Owrang.

First published November 2024 by:

Nine Arches Press
Unit 14, Sir Frank Whittle Business Centre,
Great Central Way, Rugby.
CV21 3XH
United Kingdom

www.ninearchespress.com

Printed in the United Kingdom on recycled paper by:
Imprint Digital

Nine Arches Press is supported using public funding
by Arts Council England.

Supported using public funding by
ARTS COUNCIL
ENGLAND

Contents

Part One

'What if change comes and we find ourselves unable?'

– Binyavanga Wainaina,
  One Day I Will Write About This Place

how do we live

we live with our parents and our siblings
and our grandparents
and when our siblings get married
our siblings' spouses
and when they have children
our nieces and nephews
and if we leave our home country
we live with our parents and siblings
and our grandparents
or maybe one grandparent comes to stay
when the other one passes away
or we live in houses
next door to one another
or else we live as a nuclear family
without any family nearby
so it is phone calls
that keep extended family together
in the seventies and eighties
when lines home are bad
you have to shout to be heard
and then in the nineties
phones become cordless
but the charge goes quickly
and later when skype comes in
you are frozen your face is frozen
it's how you spend your formative years
growing up listening to parents
on the phone to relatives
you sit in front of the television
watch sitcoms with one ear
on a phone conversation
that your mother is having
under the exhaust in the kitchen
while watching an object

being fought over by actors
in a studio in los angeles
your eldest brother starts
school with no english
your youngest brother starts
school with no urdu
that is the tug-of-war you know
your mother unable to have
a private conversation without
your father's mother hovering nearby
which grandparents came
and which didn't who is stuck
caring for parents not their own
is the plot you inherit
when you leave home
you are a bachelor too old
too riddled with family you live
with only one person a boyfriend
who now calls your name
from another room
with something to say or to show
or to ask or none of the above
maybe he just wants to love you
and after the fumble
you will both sleep and you will glean
in the late light what comes from
memories what is on the horizon
the shaking of plants
out of the ground
the untangling of roots
a speck of earth in your eye
frozen for a moment
lives blurry combined cleared
destined for another country
gone as you wake

subtitles

you pick it up as you go / memorise the incidents / someone says
the word at home

at school your french teacher wears a canary-yellow shirt / too bright?
he asks the class / you nod / he puts on his jacket

your uncle had a moustache that covered his lips / he lived by himself
in london in the seventies

had he gone to bars? had he gone to baths? / samuel delany asks of a man
he knew in his youth

you walk down the street of pubs of men / ready with your babble

the look that a man gives another man / the look that means a man's
weakness

you head home / unable to brave those eyes / you sit down to dinner
with your parents

the language they speak / the language of couplet and qawwali /
the language of poetic recital

another tenderness is possible / you want to say / the look that two
men might exchange / the look that means i am going to have you

not hungry? your mother asks / you nod / swallow your words /
watering love

in bed / when you are able to fall asleep / you dream in the language

you dream in the language all the time / without speaking a word of it

What is your language?

It is

Ur like the English say err is human
du as in do you speak English?

it is

I for the open mouth,   Í to note
the open mouth should be rounded
so not err in fact but oor

it is

the French word for our language
Ourdou, which seems closer
but o u r is our, already swooped up by English

it is

oo   windows on a plane, faces inside
          my parents, newly in England

it is

the town by the Ouse
where my parents put down

it is

Urdu with an English mouth
English with an Urdu mouth

it is

a brown mouth
no matter the words coming out

it is

an eddying speech
coming out at dinner

it is

oo   the reaction

it is

gag and gulp
plate and pluck

it is

the spores of a mouth
paused on a page

it is

...the name of the sound
and the sound of the name
The Nag Hammadi

it is

the question at the border
the start of the country

it is

the most beautiful language for poetry

اُردُو

the answer my parents give

Self-Portrait With Family

It's on a shelf with a globe
that photo of our parents and us
in the park in 1984.

We're the children overclothed.
Our parents were cold
so the children born in England must be also.

No one smiles. It was not the thing at the time
for my parents to smile in photos.
The Urdu word for *thing* is cheez.

My parents wear the colours of an airmail letter.
They look fashionably serious:
sunglasses and scarves; coats and gloves.

A copy of the photo was sent back to India to show
the success of moving countries, married life,
arrangement, instruction

– our grandparents' achievements.

*

I grow out of the shot
into the chat of a guy who asks
  do you have pics

I send some bare torso
with bearded chin.
We share details of likes, positions.

It is the inverse and reflection,
the life away from parental eyes
passed down.

   *

around the time of the photo
we were stopped on the street
             by a group of men
it happened a few times
       they wanted to scare us
nothing happened,
                    my parents say.

I nurse a drink in a bar, wait for the man who I know by phone alerts. He will be about a head taller than me, bigger. No one knows our arrangement. He knows my proclivities but the photo isn't chemistry. We are meeting to check if we live up to our promise.

He has asked where I'm from. I told him where my parents are from. I had an ex-boyfriend who didn't care who I was. He had gone out with a lot of brown men. For him Urdu did not mean anything. When we went on holiday he couldn't understand landscapes, why I would take a photo with no one in it. Did every beautiful place need a beaming face to obscure it?

*

What would it be if the photo sent back to india
was one with trees and grass alone
just the park in 1984 without us parents children
the note at the back of the photo might have read
this is the park in the town
meaning this is where we have walked
with the children in arms
meaning this is where we were first spotted
by those who wanted us to go

meaning here are the trees
that have gone through a season fully-leaved
sounding like the sea does
when the wind runs through them
the tall trees that have been brittle in winter
nearly wrecked by some anomalous storm

there is where we might have stood
a wavering family
fully-leaved brittle anomalous
wrapped in our boldest colours
in the knowledge that we would
only be seen from a distance

nice legs mahmood

i said and the astroturf blushed
we were boys in jogging bottoms
and he wasn't and that's what i meant
pointing my hockey stick / half-knighting
those bare legs / shorts to grey socks and
white trainers / a whistle to the warm-up

we ran one lap / him into local government
i saw in the paper / did he win / unknown
by anyone i would know now / men
with their own blushes and flourishes
towels of memory about the nape
of a warm summer's evening

stuck to the theatre while we prepare
for another stagger home / after knighting
in full the actor playing ben and joe and stan
words spoken an ambiguous preference
another group passing / i know that urdu
not directed at me but words can curve

to me alone and not in this pitched huddle
of reviewers / until i go home with sleep
apnea / who does his own laps bare legged
during the night / the water thief / dangling
singularity / unaware of the criss cross
words earlier this evening / oh my desis

i'm with a man who matches our parents
in tea consumption / and knows india through
hotels and a history of middle-class boys unafraid
to walk through a five-star lobby to his room
unsurprising the appeal of a tall broad
white man / the top of the heap in all halves

i'll never sleep with this injustice
tangled with desire and temperature and
comment rolling into my head from years ago
who wants realism / who wants romanticism
who wants me to take the bones out
of their soul / you know i saw someone

on a train eating an apple / munch mush
common enough / yet uninhibited
by the unpopular core / woody button to
collar / only the stalk forsworn / branch tip
grip provided to dangle this sinful world

Templates

'Coming Out: An Occasional Series on Personal Experiences' appeared as a feature in *Gay News*. The entries below lists each feature's date followed by its section headings.

10 April 1975
No headings

17 July 1975
No headings

23 July 1975
Work-mates
Penfriends

14 August 1975
Closetted days
Daring novel
Uncomfortable, yet cosy
Truth about me

25 September 1975
No headings

23 October 1975
Lonely
Reactions
Out is right

20 November 1975
True to myself
On the job
Worthwhile
Relatives

29 January 1976
Straight all that year
Rock band
Brut on my armpits
Oomph

11 March 1976
Preferable to treason
Nail polish
Elderly spinster
Necking

11 April 1976
The awful truth
Withering look
Guide-lines
Teaser
Two-pronged method

13 January 1977
Quicksand
Closest 'friend'
Easy way out
White lies

16 June 1977
Like laser beams
Rather fickle
My own funeral
Under the coffee table
Final condemnation
Burned the most witches

20 October 1977
Youth leader
Parents never suspected
Didn't believe me
No difference

1 June 1978
Lovers
Dead end
Boyfriends & skirts
Awkward questions
'Miss, are you...?'

Postscript:

Further articles and interviews are planned, but we welcome additional contributions from our readers.

What language do you speak at home?

The telephone is how
blood keeps track of blood

out of touching distance. With each ring
I hear your blood pressure rising.

Just leave it, I say.
I cannot not get it, you say.

Hello, then *Salaam Walaikum.*
Your names mean sacrifice and faith,

brightness and bravo. I listen in: I know
ghar is the word for house and home in Urdu.

Gharbar is the word for din and disturbance.
The house or home barged into.

There's a distinction between g and gh.
Gharbar could be garbar so unrelated to house and home.

Who can I ask about it but you?
I flit in and out of rooms, practise my g's.

A way to say gay in Urdu is *I like men,*
which seems gentler than *I'm gay* –

gay is unambivalent, angrezi, angry.
To practise Urdu is to go against the grain

into tradition. You ring off. I come out to you.
This is in 2004. There are cousins, in-laws, with us

at home. No space at the dinner table.
We're the diaspora's fodder.

You stroke the shiny cutlery.
I say to you that I shouldn't

rush into this, that I'm actually unsure.
I finish my meal, beside you.

Now since coming out, I have a boyfriend,
a man without a second tongue

I haven't told you about.
His name is from the war god.

Open the windows in his bedroom
and there's the smell of the chicken place

a street away. The tang of salt, of skin.
Alone under his roof,

I pore over his conquests.
I travel from home to his house

and back, a pendulum. At home, the phone rings.
Just leave it, I say. *I cannot not get it*, you say.

Hello then *Salaam Walaikum*.
You are worried what the wider family will say,

what faces in your dreams will say.
It's a battle of wills, a friend says

having called up the company drilling the street
outside her house. It's midnight.

She hangs up.
The language we speak at home goes

to ground. The language we speak
at home answers to ghosts.

The language we speak at home waits
for word. If I was to come out again –

pride dissuades me.
I picture the first time, fold.

Barthes says in *Camera Lucida,*
I refuse to inherit anything

from another eye than my own.
Well, I refuse to inherit anything

from my own, I observe.
I have devoted decades to this

balance of calls,
like it is a poem. *Soono,*

main aapko kuch bolna hain,
I might say. Leave it.

Soono, main aapko kuch bolna hain,
I might say. And my boyfriend

would have no idea what I'm saying.
And you would wonder why I'm picking out

those words with that same ring,
less adept to the sun.

Praying

We move closer
As more men enter
Stand shoulder to shoulder

Say our lines together
In rows raise our hands
Put them to our knees

Men of all ages
Kneeling upright bent over
Foreheads to the ground

We rise and fall
Wait by the bar
The swell of men

As it gets busier
We shuffle closer
Scent of ourselves

Songs above our heads
Men mouthing words
Approaching each other

Alone with our devotion
Waiting to be found
Praying for his love

In terms of cottaging

Your friend took his lunch,
sandwiches,
down to the public toilets.
That's gross, I said. But then I said
I wasn't coming over
because I had a throat infection.
At school F and I played a game
where F would stand on a toilet
and I would guess which stall he was in.
P copied the Eternal album for me.
He asked me, Don't you love
Don't Make Me Wait?
At home a tap was opened
downstairs. My parents argued.
They should not have been married
but were. It was arranged.
It was better to cut to the chase
and work at a relationship.
I imagined what might have been for them.
Briefly, in a toilet. Young, flush
and done with each other.
No hello goodbye. Not even sandwiches.
Just the life of a fuck
or the fuck of one's life,
bracketed by cubicle walls,
by the chorus of urinals
open-mouthed and unsurprised.

Post-independence studies (I)

The footage is from the late nineteen forties:
the camera labelled British Pathé swings onto a view
over country, trees in the foreground in the breeze,

then there's traffic flowing under an arched gate,
the famous monument with four minarets in the distance.
A close-up of the Nizam is next, the man to decide if his state

will join the newly-independent Indian dominion,
and there are scenes afterwards of street-side industry,
a trio of smiths raising their hammers almost in union.

Beyond the final shot of the reel, the state was split
and my parents' generation shrank, left for the West –
by then Hyderabad had long been condensed to a city,

the territory merged into neighbouring states, disappeared
into another family, something my mother knew.
In England, in the early nineteen seventies,

a crowd spilled out of a cinema when it was still light.
My parents stood in that audience, adjusting
to the temperature. They made their cautious way

back to their hospital accommodation flat,
where my mother began a generous letter home
and, across from her at the kitchen table, my father sat

unquestioningly sticking photos into an album given
to the bride and groom as a wedding present.
A photo showed generations of men,

formally dressed, arranged in rows. It was said
that my father's family tree began with the prophet,
so each man wore a grave look and a fez on their head

in front of the house where the occasion
of the Nizam's singular, mythic visit
hung among other pictures on a wall like an icon.

Between each page of the album lay a sheet
of tracing paper that crackled as you turned it –
the thawing sound between verses, or the folding beat

of each verse itself – a drum's pale skin.
The distance between Hyderabad and Delhi
was greater than that between London and Berlin

yet Indian was as far as the geographical description
went for our family in England. My parents moved
from one town to another, from accommodation

to a house of their own. From our front window
you could see the daily stream of children heading to school,
the flow of names and noise, the line I would follow.

fainter

after i came out my father said
You can have that sort of sex with a woman
i looked across at my mother
i wanted to say *Stop Enough*
i didn't want any more exposure.
perhaps he thought coming out was
a question to answer,
a way for men to bond
rather than declaration or prayer.

when my father was a boy
he tried to erase a bad mark on a report card
tore the paper.
when he showed the report to his father
my father collapsed.
coming out was the twist in reply
the smack of the floor
the fissure as aperture.
red-faced
my father came to england
where two indian woman took him for
white, his proudest story,
a legend among his wider family
where everyone married a degree of cousin.

he had a weights bench in the garage
where he threatened to make us sleep
when we behaved badly as children. our father –
whose arms were larger than his in the house?
i never learned how to translate fear
into fearsomeness. that was my queerness.

i sleep with a man i call dad who calls me son,
an immigrant to this country
but from the opposite direction to my parents.
no trembling family of his own.
in bed one spring afternoon
in the time he can get away from
the care he gives his dying father
we hug each other tight, let go,
over and over. *this feels so good,* he says,
his ear against mine.
i've needed this for such a long time.

ancestry

after i came out my mother said
why did you choose this
i said that i didn't choose it
but why are you making it
so difficult for yourself
why would i make it so
difficult for myself i asked her
yes why would you she said
i said because i hadn't chosen it
had she chosen being straight
could she choose being gay
yes i could my mother said
i didn't know what to say to that
i didn't know what she meant
was that her coming out
i was on the other side of the table
we had eaten dinner
she was putting food into tupperware
we never spoke again about
anyone's coming out
it is difficult for me at a table
now years later
i have eaten a bag of fibre
i want to lie face down
i met a man on grindr
who came out when he was forty
he said of that earlier time
i wondered is this all there is
i told him i had three sisters
he gave me a new toothbrush
i saw him take it out of the packet
i thought of all the toothbrushes
that were handed out before me

that line of gifted lovers
ancestry that had become mine
i brushed my teeth put on my clothes
as if it was morning i thanked him
went home and made dinner
i wondered what my mother would do
if she was making this meal
how much salt she would add
how much turmeric
chili powder garlic ginger
i'm always surprised when people say
i don't eat garlic
how can you not eat garlic
if we heard such a statement
me and my mother
we would look to each other
what kind of life must it be
what possibility for pleasure
what shame
what terrible shame
it would be not to have
what made for so much joy

duas

a dua for my mother the head girl / leaving school a year
early to be married to move to england / the headmistress
announcing it at morning assembly

a dua for my mother on the phone to her family / having
to shout to be heard in the decades the lines to india were
fuzzy / my father's family looming in the next room

a dua for my mother teaching me how to make daal / hindi
pop in the background / a dua for the anorak she wears as
an apron

a dua for my mother arguing at the embassy / needing a
visa to visit her mother who is unwell / a dua for the woman
in the line who tells my mother you are lucky / the woman's
father is already with allah

a dua for the flight / a dua for the plane that lands safely

a dua for my mother with her case / meeting her brother
at arrivals / is she – ?

a dua for the chorus of strays by the airport / their tails
wagging no

a dua for the silent drive home / the roaring city

a dua for the friend who says she will wash our
grandmother's body

a dua for our mother who says no we will do it / her and
her sister

a dua for my aunt who tells my mother / why did you
say that / i didn't want to do it

a dua for a burial

a dua for when she comes back to us / our mother

a dua for when she tells us she would have chosen to be
a doctor / she wouldn't have chosen our father / she would
have chosen an earlier flight

a dua for when she tells us about her mother / she was
a straightforward woman / you could tell her anything

a dua for when she sits on the chair in her room / our
mother / the folding chair she uses only for praying /
she can't sit on the floor anymore / a dua for knees

a dua for godard's *a word is what's unsaid* / a dua for when
there's nothing but what's said

a dua for the patter of worry that wakes sleep / a dua for
the loved ones

a dua for this country dashed with another

Alifbehpehrian for extended family

١	alif	And when they visit, where will you put them?
ب	beh	Bahut means *many* in Urdu,
پ	peh	pareshan means *worry*.
ت	teh	To create mattresses, blankets will be overlaid.
ٹ	tteh	Tours will be booked. A photo will show you
ث	seh	smiling by the Tower of London.
ج	jeem	Jegga means *place* or *space*.
چ	che	Chamcha means *spoon* or *flatterer*.
ح	heh	Home will be a stage for however many days,
خ	kheh	converted space for your performance.
د	dal	Daily you will wonder if a yawn is an opinion –
ڈ	ddal	desire will be easier to judge. As host you will be
ذ	zal	zealous, bearing hot beverages, smiles
ر	reh	the reputation of your side of the family.
ز	zeh	It will zigzag the diaspora, your guests' review,
س	seen	so say you go the mosque on both Eids and
ش	sheen	show off the children's half-hearted Urdu while
ص	suad	surrendering the more comfortable armchair.
ض	zuad	At some point, the curtain will drop:
ط	toy	arguments will feel as close as snores or
ظ	zoy	movements from an adjacent bedroom.
ع	ain	A poem for the visit might be: 'Ghazal for in-laws,'
غ	ghain	'Ghazal for a long play.' The refrain will be

ف	feh	'family' or 'favourably' or 'food' or possibly
ق	kaaf	'kasam,' *oath*, or 'kasam seh,' *truthfully*, or
ک	kkaaf	'kaam' meaning *work*, or 'kirai' meaning *rent*.
گ	gaaf	Gather your options like a menu, and avoid
ل	laam	land or who is stealing whose property back home.
م	meem	'Mohabbat' means *love*, 'mehnat' is *hard work*.
ن	noon	No conversation will be as precarious,
و	vow	verbatim, as it is with family that comes to be yours.
ہ	choti heh	How gently you will tread, heaving expectation.
ھ	do chasmi heh	How late they will go to bed, leaving all the lights on.
ی	choti yeh	'You must visit us next time,' your guests will say and
ے	badi yeh	you will want your effort repaid, so you nod.

Zaban i urdu

Zaban i urdu, meaning *language of the camp*.
In Urdu, *here* or *hither* is idher or yahan.
There is udher or wahan.

    We drive through a town. My father says,
    We lived here when we first came to England.
    Temporary lodging. A street of houses low

to the ground. About returning to India,
my mother tells a cousin, *We will not go*
back there like we planned. Thither. Home's fading

    origin. Urdu from the Turkish word ordu,
    an army. Horde/order/ordu/Urdu.
    Watching *Gladiators* on TV as a boy,

I copied the pose Phoenix made before an event.
One palm by my ear, the other on my hip,
I shifted weight for my parents.

    Every year, I was sent to cricket training,
    praying my arms would fix like wickets or alifs.
    A curved line, an extravagant gesture, Sontag notes.

Also, *Camp and tragedy are antithesis.*
At deep cover, my father said
People are asking about your status,

    meaning what respectable reason
    could reach the sensitive ears of our community
    explaining this long a bachelorhood?

Dates are a problem
now with men single-minded as soldiers.
No camp in camp.

You're so butch, a renegade mocks one morning
as I roll out of his bed to head to the gym.
In the question of who is and who isn't,

the meaning shifts after headaches
and arm squeezes to hypertensive.
The doctor shows me a diagram of a heart

in which a red arrow winds, ricocheting
off sides, as it passes through.
There, there.

There is an internal, irresistible language:
a buzzword, Ramipril, to unlock
no mellow passage of blood.

I assemble grains and greens
and a running regime that takes me
on a loop of neighbourhood pavements,

trying to make as few stops
and as many gasping steps as possible,
swerving return.

next door

recently i have had cause to think of you again
neighbour why you became a door
against our faces and we held the gesture
the plate with our golden mosaic
mincemeat in pastry
diamonds of almond saffron cake
it is eid we said holding out
our translation of kitchen time
offering tessellated samosas and roat
our diligent intro we mentioned to you
we helped our mother make them
children of the house next door
deliverers of tradition in treat form
when we came home with the plate intact
tainted by your slam door trick
eat it yourselves our mother suggested
from the lineage of borders
the taste of the look you gave
oil on our lips oiled our understanding
of your glare the neighbourly air
at our skin the closed welcome
and knock of celebration
i forget i'm reminded
we were children at the threshold
pride in our people our practice
thrived in spite of your doorstep light
your withdrawal from our offer
of the crunch of filo layers
sponge with slivered almonds
legacy of ancestor tables
neighbour you missed so much treasure

Part Two

'Where is my refuge,
my fine and feathered friend?'

– 'Refuging' from *Bite Hard* by Justin Chin

Notes in the dark

1.

The film starts at a building site. A young man, high on the scaffold, makes his way down. He has seen a police car.

2.

For the first act of the film, the young man tries to get in touch with a lawyer. The film is full of phone calls, letters, overhearing. Communication fails; or it is intercepted, we discover, maliciously.

3.

The young man tells his friends he is leaving the island. But he is caught by the police before he does. The police inspector knows what is going on – that the young man is being blackmailed. The boy lies on his front in a cell. It is over.

4.

'Boy from Kenya (over 21) seeks fellow gay Kenyans for friendship, or am I the only one? Anybody else? Essex, anywhere. Box ----.' *The Pink Paper*, 27 October 1988.

5.

The police inspector, in the film, sees injustice. He says to his less forgiving colleague, 'There's no doubt that a law that sends homosexuals to prison offers unlimited opportunities for blackmail.'

6.

The young man's lawyer steps into the spotlight: he decides to find out the identity of the blackmailer.

7.

A teacher who came out to us made reference to this film, *Victim* (1961), which is why I sought it out – an heirloom.

8.

There are many stories about the police among our remaining family in India. My cousin describes being stopped by a pair of policemen. The Urdu phrase he uses translates to, 'Let's mess with him' or 'Let's have some fun.'

9.

In 2009, I accompany my mother and one of her friends to a conversation between Arundhati Roy and Shami Chakrabarti. It's the day homosexual sex is decriminalised in India. The audience cheers. I feel the reverberations, sitting next to my mother in London. But the law is overturned.

10.

The Pink Paper. Gay Times. Diva. Attitude. I am logged into the archive. I remember these magazines up on shelves: the curve of the page, fingers beneath the spine.

11.

In my breaks from the archive, I look for a date. I get a match on an app. 'Can you take a piston?' the man asks in the chat. I go to find the definition of piston beyond the one I know. *Noun:* What moves forward and back, up and down (inside a cylinder, against a liquid or gas) to produce/impart motion.

12.

'The NAZ project launches *Safer Fucking Packs* for Gay Identified Men and Men Who Have Sex With Men from the South Asian, Turkish, Arab and Irani Communities. Each Safer Fucking Pack contains: 2x Extra Thick Condoms. 2x water-based lubes. Info in community languages on how to fuck safely. And they are all FREE to you.' *The Pink Paper*, 22 December 1995.

13.

I remember my grandmother saying to my father, in our community language, when there were two men in an embrace on television, 'In Hyderabad, there were men like this. They were married, had children.'

14.

How would it have been if my parents had stayed in India? In that universe, would I have been married, become a father? But a single shift in an alternate world means the transformation of that world.

15.

Perhaps my relationship to India is something like this. For ten months or so, there was scaffolding around the buildings on my street in London. Whenever there was some kind of work, the noise of the wind rippling the plastic sheeting, a builder fiercely calling out – I would get up from my desk and go to the window.

16.

'Is it possible in India to see something happen and then not have to acknowledge it?' Pragya Singh interviewing Madhavi Menon, *Politics of Desire, Indian Cultural Forum 2019*.

17.

People are cut off from home, from their language. The government have cut ties with the young: the reminders are the dirty streets, the kids with nothing to do. The train passing by the shadowed house is the reminder of the mother who cut ties with this life. Toenails are cut; a ribbon is cut. The string holding up the curtains between the screened-off parts of life is cut. This is the world of *My Beautiful Launderette* (1985).

18.

'How could anyone in their right mind call this silly little island off Europe their home?' an auntie says to a wide-eyed Omar, the soon-to-be manager of the launderette.

19.

I have time to spend on the archive, to search through the family history of these classifieds, these reels, find the few experiences of people with masks like mine.

20.

There's much that attracts me to *My Beautiful Launderette*, but/ and I'm not Pakistani. Other than long summer trips, I have spent no extended time in India, either. I'm a visitor to the archive. I've been given a username, a password that I keep on forgetting and need to reset.

21.

In 2016, 2 in 5 LGBT people in India were blackmailed or knew someone who had been blackmailed. (Figures from The Humsafar Trust.)

22.

How might it go, that process of taking advantage of desire and coming out? *You get a match: start to chat. He asks what you like and, then, if you want to meet. Inside you the ground trembles. Compose a fib for your parents. He has sent you his address.*

23.

Drive to his place. He buzzes you in. You strip down, new to this world, almost past inexperience. Just wait, he says, stepping into the bathroom. You sit tenderly on the bed.

24.

'Leave details of your meeting with family or friends when seeing a respondent for the first time.' *Gay Scotland*, December 1996.

25.

You sit tenderly on the bed. But he emerges still clothed: shows you the footage, your eagerness, minutes ago, already the abject past. Put on your clothes. Together you walk to the ATM. Drain that account. He has your number.

26.

Drive home. How was it? your parents ask, meaning the fib.

27.

Who might be going through this now that I know? That cousin of mine? And is he scammer or scammed, what side of the coin?

28.
'Damn these stories about places you've never been to,' Omar's uncle exclaims.

29.
'If it was love why would I want to stamp it out?' the lawyer tells his wife.

30.
The photo of the lawyer and the young man burns in the fire; Omar and Johnny splash each other by the sink.

i found a man shallow

i found a man shallow / who went no deeper than the prostate / leaving him i felt such envy / all the men that would come after me / to his bed / the knock that goes *remember remember* in me goes *next next* in him / we lived in different time zones in the same city / when sex for him came to mean the possibility of a fast death my parents newly in the country were circled by a gang in the street / both of us with fright in our blood / blighted by caste / being top to him was sacred / men to him an unaccounted number / to me each prime / i want to be able to leave my bed for other beds / make it new / man to man to man / as a wasp moves from flower to flower / as if you move country without remnants / but you do decide after a time not to retire back there / desire for me daily declaration and baggy monster / picking up a man should be as casual as a white man crossing a border / gliding on ice / it should be a trip to the movies / pinky misses popcorn / badar misses trailers / kavya misses opening credits aishwarya's entrance / where is faraan / where is this switzerland sweden / let me join those syncopated lines at urinals / the gatherings on the heath / each man baring himself / our mouths honest stopped with each other

Of not going in

At 19 years old / you did go in

a spider in draining water / you were in a group of friends / none of you had been to a gay club / legs going / dancing a kind of scrambling / you were plastered with looking / you were gay but no one knew / no one resembled you / one friend made out with a guy / laughed / you felt betrayal / piped up only for water / the future would catch you between a glass & postcard / put you out

At 29 years old / you got up to the door / walked past

friends had started to get married / light-footed / you went to weddings / came back parched / mindful of feet / you walked down the street / swerved past the intended bar / you became a walker / the flâneur was avoider / tangling only with route-making / you walked london / aesthete of asceticism / plenty of things in the world didn't happen / you lay with your pathology

At 39 years / oh this is getting silly

maybe it is agoraphobia or arachnophobia / fear of the self / are you scared of blood or dark rooms or ghosts / which is homophobia / walk through the door & there will probably be men mundanely drinking / white men with their eyes on you / at home your parents put the quran on the topmost shelf / fearlessness was in reach / with your people

At 43

now you are able to go into a queer bookshop / search
out a dictionary / are you gay if you don't go out / you
meet a friend / you are pressed between pages / your
fate is friends who return books as they were lent / now
even those bars those clubs have shut down moved on /
your inability has become obsolete / consider the spider
& the web / you protested marriage but believed in the
institution of the gay bar

At 47

a fading story / you go in finally / foreign body / consider
the flood plain / life become its coping mechanisms /
blame the safety of desks / & distances / familiar faces
/ oh snap out of it / remember what elsa sang / let time
be queer / remember what the quran said / allah made
your homes a place of rest / you sit on a slide's summit
/ you are here / older / odder / spider / when will you
be back

Translations

'The city became more colourful and diverse, which is great. The city became also, in parts of it, more conservative, aggressive towards differences. We are now in a situation that there is quite a bit of violence instigated against 'us' by youngsters with a migration background. And on the other hand we have politicians in the left wing and liberal politicans [who] don't know how to tackle the problem because they are also afraid to discriminate.' – Ernst Verhoeven, co-organiser of First Amsterdam Pride Parade, in a spoken interview in 2021.

'...to be less literal, more poetic; less inhibited, more playful; less logical, more personal.' – Tiffany Tsao, *Beyond the Binary – A Note on Translating.*

1.

The city became
more colourful and diverse,
which is great.

The city became also,
in parts of it,
more conservative, aggressive

towards differences. We are now
in a situation that there is quite a bit
of violence instigated against 'us'

by youngsters with a migration
background. And on the other hand
we have politicians in the left wing

and liberal politicians [who] don't know
how to tackle the problem because
they are also afraid to discriminate.

2.

he/i/it/be/came/a/am/me
or/ore/colour/our/land/a/an/dive/i/ive/verse
hi/i/his/i/is/eat/a/at

he/i/it/be/came/a/am/me/meal/a/so
i/par/a/art/part/so/fit/i/it
or/ore/on/vat/a/at/i/ive/a/i/ive

to/war/wards/a/i/if/ere/wear/ear/no
i/sit/it/at/on/hat/at/here/ere/i/tea/i/it
i/i/in/i/gate/at/ate/a/again/gain/a/i/in/

you/young/wit/i/ham/i/rat/a/at/i/on
back/a/ground/round/a/don't/he/her/and
a/politic/i/tic/i/i/a/an/sin/i/he/win/i

a/i/era/a/politic/i/i/i/a/an/do/no/ow
tot/tack/a/let/he/rob/be/cause/a/use
he/a/real/a/so/a/raid/a/aid/i/is/rim/im/i/i/in/at/ate

3.

he/i/it/be/came/a/am/me
or/ore/colour/our/land/a/an/dive/i/ive/verse
hi/i/his/i/is/eat/a/at

he/i/it/be/came/a/am/me/meal/a/so
i/par/a/art/part/so/fit/i/it
or/ore/on/vat/a/at/i/ive/a/i/ive

to/war/wards/a/i/if/ere/wear/ear/no
i/sit/it/at/on/hat/at/here/ere/i/tea/i/it
i/i/in/i/gate/at/ate/a/again/gain/a/i/in/

you/young/wit/i/ham/i/rat/a/at/i/on
back/a/ground/round/a/don't/he/her/and
a/politic/i/tic/i/i/a/an/sin/i/he/win/i

a/i/era/a/politic/i/i/i/a/an/do/no/ow
tot/tack/a/let/he/rob/be/cause/a/use
he/a/real/a/so/a/raid/a/aid/i/is/rim/im/i/i/in/at/ate

4.

and liberal politicians [who] don't know
how to tackle the problem because
they are also afraid to discriminate.

[   ] to correct/streamline
[   ] to enclose/separate as
[   ] extra/explanatory
[   ] omission/fluency
[   ] what is unsaid in a public space
[   ] to hold ellipsis
[to hold hands]
[Türkçe]
[اَلْعَرَبِيَّةُ]

6.

'The narrative of progress for gay rights is thus built on the back of racialized others, for whom such progress was once achieved, but is now backsliding or has yet to arrive.' Jasbir Puar

'Queers, no longer a threat to the nation's moral and cultural fabric, now become bodies in need of saving or protecting from the Muslim or Arab other, whose actual or potential victimhood justifies the war on terror.' Drew Paul

'Every misfortune that befalls the earth, or your own persons, is ordained before We bring it into being. That is easy enough for God; so that you may not grieve for the good things you miss, or be overjoyed at what you gain.' *The Quran* (Al-Hadid [Iron] 57:23)

7.

To translate what is said in public
is to make one's own narrative fabric
is to find new ways towards arriving
streamlining what is separate
what is omitted now become bodies
needing saving or protecting from.

To not hide anymore to hold one's head up
to march to make space walk in pride
to not be afraid to find one's tribe
to be overjoyed to hold up signs
shove it in their faces to see the looks
on their faces a face you don't like
to look out for to look daggers at
to not be afraid to call out
report recount narrate
discriminate.

8.

There a re those who see translation li ke the enemy at the ramparts. Y our

parents always told you t o watch out for your own. The prickly texture of pride.

To flag. How to be alert to those who co ndemn violence murder as a rus e to

direct hate against those w ho are here. How to stitch that [ ] lack of surprise.

to look daggers at to not be afraid to call out report recount

the looks on their faces a face you don't like to look out for

to be overjoyed to hold up signs shove it in their faces see

make spa ce walk in pride to not be afraid to find one's tribe

To not hide anymo re to hold one's head up to march to

A Complaint

Did you submit it yet? you asked.
No, I said. I was a junior staff member,
fairly new. I feared the complaint itself
would colour my reputation, possibilities
for promotion. I described my complaint to
other friends and family who found it mundane:
reporting it would change nothing.
When I told you, you said you would
put it online immediately. I made you stop.
We were among a race, the English,
for whom lack of complaint brought respect.
You want invisibility, you said.
Another friend asked me if I wanted revenge.
I needed a salary and, in the future,
a larger salary. *What would you like to be*
the outcome of your complaint?
the form asked. I wrote a poem about it:
one version went through the motions
of the incident; another obliquely referred to it.
There was a sonnet in a crown of sonnets
that concluded, *It is a stream of stops*
I progress with, a consciousness of margins,
a movement of halts. I went home after work,
did calisthenics by the sofa. Every day,
I would see the men who locked their doors
when I was nearby. One day, I saw you
by chance, out in the world. I thought you would
want to talk about it so I did not call out, wave
my arms, distinguish myself from the crowd.

Self-Portrait With Stops

1.

We were students at an LGBT icebreaker
in 2003. Across the room I saw a man
whose name had the same ending as mine.
He told me that he had written a letter
to his family that was found by his brother.
What happened next? I asked, but then
it was play time, what might have been
preparation, a chorus line. We stood on chairs:
we had to order ourselves alphabetically
without touching the floor of the union.
We weaved past one another, asking names
across the intimacy of ledges.

2.

I came out and a year after went away
to live in a town in the east of England.
The walk to the university campus took me
past a house where two boys yelled a word
over a fence that brought out my skin.
A man called them in, their father I presume.
I did not turn, walked on. I wanted to be
surrounded by family. Like the boys, I also
followed what my watchful father had said:
after coming out I had circled back,
had said I was not, lowering my head
behind the shelter of home's boundary.

3.

Weeks later, I walked in the other direction
at night, from campus back to my house.
On the cycle barriers across a path sat
two teenage boys. One held a hammer.
Check your reflexes, he said, aiming for
my knees as I walked past. I began to run,
did not stop until my house. After that
I took school's out as my curfew. I was ten
years older than these kids, a shadow
of them – brave neighbourhood faces
not practised enough to keep feelings
tucked away like a stone in a pocket.

4.

A decade later, rush hour delays in London:
a pair of policemen wait after the barriers
and stop me to look through my bag, to ask
where I'm going, what I do for work.
Commuters step over headlines, glance back
at the timeliness of my unshaved face:
I mark myself on a list of ethnicities.
Those years of terror, I gave my thanks
without flinching, zipped pockets neatly,
tried to walk from dubious to unremarkable.
Amid the rows of desks in the office
it was the immoderate who was admired,
the line crosser, the rule breaker, to move
into a world that you wanted or wanted you.

5.

And those stop-start days I was learning how to
walk into a gay pub or bar, order a drink and be
comfortable with men around me. I stared hard
out of the window. A woman waved at me
from across the street: I had two glasses and left
which I called queer success. *Check your reflexes.*
By the river I met up with a man who told me
he had told his family he was gay at fifty only
after he had attended a self-help conference
where all the participants were encouraged to
walk barefoot down a path of hot coals
to show that they could do anything.

6.

In another bar the leader of a trio
of brown boys with patchy beards
came over to ask *What's happening here?*
because we shared a resemblance and
he was keen to roll out his judgment
regarding the empties before me.
At that point my date, a white man,
came to the table with another round
and as he began to talk about what
I don't recall, all I remember was the trio
who vanished suddenly at his presence and
his obliviousness to what he had stopped,
as if there was nothing to dismissing
those who wanted to keep you close.

7.

Perhaps it's unsurprising to you as it came to be
or what I should have expected coming from
a house called out of order that I was taken
aside often when I landed at Immigration,
questioned, told to find and unlock my bag.
The guard would root through my suitcase
wearing gloves, lift out a book and ask me
to explain the contents. My literature
teachers never mentioned such a circumstance
for interpretation. We were pupils of the texture
of words, trained with pages stripped of titles,
free of biography. You would attempt a first class
reading of the extract without recourse to a name
and, a week later, have a red light appear at the corner
of the keyboard when they scanned your passport
against which your words paled, suspect, useless.

To the beat

Aslama, vb. – to submit. Muslim, n. – one who submits.

To submit to what happens
between pen and paper.
Submit from *mittere*,
the Latin word for *to send*.
Mittee means earth
in Urdu, my poorly inherited language.
The missing *r* makes for a new route:
submit are hands filtering soil,
estimating the composition underfoot.

Going down to the prayer mat as a child –
praying alongside my sisters and mother
in the space between her bed and the wall –
my nose touched the soft mat
when we put our foreheads to the ground.
Then came the laughs, irresistible,
when one of us banged the wall with a foot.

Submitting is the nose stroke,
the wall's godly reply. It is
Many thanks and best wishes –
lowdown, accommodating,
often ironic. Submit is the finality
of a submit button: see the error
only after you hand in the thesis.
Hear the ringing phone's harshness,
by which a clarity grows.
At what point will you be done,
say, *No more, I resign*?
Submission is the tenderness
of orientation. The chorus
of cower, struggle, arousal.
You watch the luscious evening,

fingers tendril around a notebook.
Submit to the form – the elemental
submission, like a leaf on the wind.
So begin your dance on the air.

Presentation

When we meet in person and both know what
we have said in our chats about what we would
like to do together, now comes the time to do it.
Here I am fleshed out, standing on your doorstep,
the beginning's end, the end of deferral. But still
there are clothes to drop, our crosshatch of beards,
the way you do this or that and of course the sputters,
finales, exhales. I come home. I take a nap and dream
and wake to two messages, one from you,
another from my mother who says my father is
steadily reducing the number of pots in the garden
so could I come next weekend to help him upturn
the really heavy ones, the ones that sit like boulders?
Those plants need to be restored to the earth so when
I do go home a week later, for the first time in ages
the inside of pots touch air and I angrily tell my parents
not to embark on these physical projects, my voice
righteous, raw. But they want things settled now.
It's that time. Can I understand?

                                    You there mister?
comes your message while I'm on the train, and I can't
stand the there-ness as I head back to the city, the only
others in my carriage a group of sunburned men.
We have noted each other. I desire a shell, an ear porcelain-
smooth into which I can slip and only hear the crashing
waves. I adjust my mask at my stop. The doors beep
before opening and a man yells, *Aller hoo Ackbaar!*
The old insult. British in inflection. I'm sure they can
smell me. The train takes them: *relief, relief.* I count
fourteen hours until I'm due back at my desk so I shift
into professional mode. At home, I work on a presentation,

a bid for which I am not sure of the priority, if it's just
money the clients want, or flattery, or a scapegoat,
while outside on the path a pigeon lands, grey and black,
iridescent at the neck, curious, cautious, oblivious,
staccato, chancing, escaping – *That's where I will finish.*
Thank you. Are there any questions, thoughts?

References

From my window I see him
Burgundy Shirt who rang the doorbell
My mother's colleague who taught IT

The first out gay man in our house
I did not fancy him / We both wore glasses
He had a goatee / Smelled sweaty

As he sat in front of our computer
That had slowed unbearably / My fault maybe
Weight of videos of men pounding piled

My mother opened a window
There's nothing I can do about it
Her colleague said / Meaning his scent

As a family we shaved ourselves of odours
So you wouldn't catch us
The only Asian family for a few streets

I had questions that blanched
While he took the machine back to zero
Re-uploaded all the programmes

Did he know the sites I searched?
Had he visited them too? / At school
One teacher would say when another was away

Mr C is out today / It was a joke
(Mr C was gay) / Some pupils got it
Like my friend who I passed

On Old Compton Street twenty years later
With his boyfriend / Palms together
Queer how we had never asked it of each other

We were schoolboys with careful looks
Studying elders we couldn't claim
Even as men / We didn't say *Hi* on the street

I went the house of a man past retirement
Who said *gay* under his breath as opera played
I declined dinner / But swallowed his seed

My references are hunched
I sit with men twenty years my senior
Who describe the time I was learning words

As a youth put into deep freeze
A fence around affection
A story of self-protection slippery to recount

A prospective partner's calls left unanswered
As another friend who counselled the newly sick
Encountered him in his clinic

My men are guards coughing at the gate
What training have they had / What colours
Their shifts / What wars at touch

I sat with my mother's colleague
Hands over the grey keys
The monitor a bulky box that cracked

If you tried to move it / The console
As large as a drawer on its side
It was a right state wasn't it he said

That's false / I forget how we concluded
If he took note of me at all / (I wanted him to)
Even one's own story is a surfeit

I bear witness

I loved reading and so I wrote versions of the books I had read.
It took a long time until I realised that I needed to live a life
to write something novel.

I met Tom East London whose real name was David,
an audiotician who knew how sounds travelled through buildings.
Before we went into his house he greeted his neighbour
and I worried whether what we said in bed would fly
out the window to their ears. We needed privacy and air.

Afterwards I saw the small dampnesses,
the tinged stains unknowingly made on the bedsheet.
Rise O Days from your fathomless depths, Whitman writes.

At school once, a boy larger than me sat in my lap,
made sounds as a pornstar would. I couldn't get the boy off,
only by grabbing at his crotch.
The weight of that boy: a lug, a log. I walked off,
left the laughing crowd. I don't remember where.
The memory drops off.

Often me and my sisters went with my mother to a halal butchers
on the other side of town. I would never see my schoolmates there.

At the back of the shop
the owner's nephew cut meat using the electric saw.
At the front of the shop
there were crates of vegetables and fruits.

The owner handed me and my sisters a lollipop
each, which we chewed and swallowed.
We would then suck the sticks and leave them in our pockets,
in the grooves of the armrests of the car.

My mother would find them, these secrets.
I couldn't hide from her. She could look at me and say
You are unwell and I would nod.

I went to hospital to get my tonsils removed.
When was that: 1988, 1989? I was a child of the eighties.
I was getting to know songs in the charts.
What is the depth at which knowing ends and fathoming starts?

My mother has since told me in a train station car park
and quietly while my father is in the next room
or when he has gone to bed.

Gay men with white and dyed hair whose company I seek
have told me with slim-necked glasses in their hands,
bloody lips.

My father whispered to me when I was born that
There is no god but Allah and Mohammed is his prophet.
It was an initiation into memory-making and line-making
and murmur-making, into the betrayal I feel to all
the others in my life when I say I love you to one snoring brute.

Rise O Days, whispered, waved.
From what abandoning empires do we, do we not surface?

At school we learned how to save a friend floating in water.
We held onto our partner's chin, scooped beneath our bodies,
tugged them to an end.

When we reached land,
we came alive, switched places,
began again.

Ghazal for an Older Man

To map the city through the long-resisted calls of a body
drawn to the lined architectures of the body.

A house for the gentry, each room now a home, in what was
the scullery his bed and the hot, creamy-white of his body.

A train out to the incense flat, a rite, he put on a cock ring
from a wooden box next to an icon of Mary with Christ's body.

During a special in the apex of the city, you held on, kept clear
of a plastered biopsy on the neck of his high-flying body.

By his fish tank, your neighbour, grumpy that you didn't initiate,
showed you a sculpture on his phone, knocked as his own body.

You are versed in twinges, lost youths, claims to immutability.
It is a couplet when a body lies beside, listens to, another body.

On a shelf of trinkets there's you, boy, in his travelogue pages,
leather-bound records of dusk and your namesake's body.

In a blue bubble he writes that he will be caring for his father,
so these next weeks he cannot be with another wanting body.

The nutty one who chews licorice root to grow his hair calls you,
he is searching the shops for a pistachio polo to fit his body.

What do you do? You bounce off a kiss and bound down the street
to meet the station gate and the taste, again it comes, of his body.

You're A, initially, who yearns not to stay, hitched to verses,
lateness, endings and the long-standing enclosures of the body.

Post-independence studies (II)

In memoriam Martyn

Variations of light provide a route through these years,
how we fell into a dating routine, meeting outside your work,
heading to the nearby pub for a couple of beers

and then back to your workplace, an anonymous
building, closed for the night. In via the service lift,
we walked across a floor of empty desks to your office

where we removed our clothes and you'd need
to pee always after we had messed around for a bit.
While you were gone, I sat on the floor, worried

and icy in your office, considering what I would do
if you didn't come back – through the windows came
the orange streetlight, the only illumination. Years after you,

a boyfriend would leave a lamp on low by the bedside
before sliding under the duvet. I remember his cold hands –
he told me that he felt relief when his father died,

that he wouldn't have to come out to him. He had been
to Hyderabad for work, knew it fairly well, pronounced it
high-dera-bad after HITEC City, a place I had not seen.

I met you again. You took me to a club
where white men shone like teeth under a UV light.
I held my drink, turning green-eyed, looking at emails

on my phone, waiting for you who described
the fuck bar as a utopian space. You went off
with a tall man almost as soon as we arrived –

I had just handed my rucksack and jacket
to the cloakroom attendant who in return gave me
a goody bag of condom and lube in a clear packet.

Above the bar, porn was playing on a screen.
I recognised the actors who embraced in a pool,
balanced on a sun lounger in the next scene.

I sat on a red chair, or a white chair under a red light.
A man walked past wearing no clothes. An advert
appeared on the screen for Underwear Night,

then came the trailer for the club: the street over
our heads and a man who represented us, naïve, silent,
stepping through the unmarked door for a lover.

time and place

my father cuts up his food into tiny pieces
puts it into a box adds water puts it in the fridge
eats it days later we don't know why he does this

we ask him to describe where he is when he calls us
remembering the number but not his location
he has left the house from under our noses

can you describe what's around you we ask
there's a street there's a shop there's a
building with a man sitting at a desk

who needs to get better at dealing with stress
the a/c in the office switches off at 6pm
and it is terribly quiet you can hear

your colleagues make the gentlest sigh
the ones that remain at the end of the day
before you leave to go to an ex's house

with a bottle of gin and a notion of a life
do you want to grow old together
you ask as he empties his glass

your ex who tells his new partner
after you go about your visit
the new partner who takes an evening class

every tuesday learning a new language
topics including food and drink
family and work greetings and farewells

our age

for years, on scattered weekends
in suburban houses or local halls
our community reunites to celebrate
oversee bismillahs, retirements
the inheritance of friendships
my father drives us to a house
where we meet his and our mother's friends
and the children of the friends
and we go to the children's rooms
to play board games or video games
and when lunch is ready
we sit around the dining table
while the adults ask us questions
about our performances at school

and years later, older with jobs
living away from our parents
we meet the friends
unknown to our school friends
again at a community event where
we're told about the wedding we missed
and the boy who squirms at introduction
I help my father as he gets up from a chair
or when he doesn't hear what someone asks
I accompany my mother
when she asks me to meet
a former neighbour visiting England
conversation filters through
salaam alaikum, walaikum salaam

I don't speak outside the direction of the day
of the apps in which each faceless man
writes in the chat *can you accom*
i can't accom instead I listen to talk
of 1961, 1971, those initial years
of arrival, novelty, conservatism
looking for a shred of heat for skin and mouth
a street unperturbed by proximity
I crave a visit to an unknown address
where a guy honest and horny
will say he can only come after I do
and the way he looks at me with willing eyes
I wonder if this meeting might be repeated
whether I could share with him

the chronicle of those ill-fitting reunions
the occasional marks in the calendar
at the end of a table of dates
what was dull for us and vital
as another child for our parents
the divergence of the hours
driving back from a community party
everyone tired of faces, attracted to roadsides
myself or my brother or sister graduated
to the wheel, our parents now our passengers
asleep to a ghazal soundtrack
a harmonium opening, a tabla joining
music we'd replace with radio
turning the dial towards or away

Acknowledgements

Thank you to the editors of the following publications where versions of these poems were published: *Ambit, Bath Magg, Harana Poetry, Magma, Oxford Poetry, Perverse, Poetry Birmingham, Poetry London, Poetry Review, The Rialto, Wild Court* and *100 Queer Poems* (Vintage Books, 2022).

In the epigraph to 'Translations', Ernst Verhoeven's comments are taken from a BBC News interview, broadcast 8 August 2021; 'Beyond the Binary – A Note on Translating' by Tiffany Tsao appeared in *Sergius Seeks Bacchus* (2019, Tilted Axis Press) by Norman Erikson Pasaribu. In part 8 of 'Translations', Jasbir Puar's words are taken from the article 'Rethinking Homonationalism' in the *International Journal of Middle East Studies 45*, May 2013; Drew Paul's words appeared in the article 'Impossible Figures: Reorienting Depictions of Gay Palestinians' in *A Journal of Lesbian and Gay Studies* 27(4), October 2021.

'Notes in the dark' refers to the LGBT Magazine Archive. The British Pathé film that opens 'Post-independence studies (I)' is titled 'Hyderabad Still Has To Settle Its Future (1947)'.

Thank you to my friends, to all at Nine Arches Press and to the Ledbury Poetry Critics. I owe a great many thanks to Prue Bussey-Chamberlain and Jane Commane for their time, support and close reading of these poems.

Thank you to my family – Babi, Minoo, Munni, Faizi, Shaan.